Cyber Security

Understand Hacking and Protect Yourself and Your Organization From Ever Getting Hacked

By: Hacking Studios

Table of Contents

Introduction

Congratulations for downloading this book, and thank you for doing so. Cyber security, the practice of protecting yourself online, is of the utmost importance in today's digital, technologically advanced world. Both individuals and companies are at risk of having a hacker break into their computer systems and cause extensive damage. This damage includes but is not limited to identity theft, fraudulent financial transactions, significant financial loss, infection with viruses and other forms of malware, manipulation and/or deletion of data, and any other number of things that can wreak havoc on your personal life or your business.

Fortunately, there are a lot of things that you can do to protect yourself online. Most people are not aware of these things, thereby leaving themselves open to hackers. However, if you are reading this book, you are probably somebody who wants to know what you can do in order to keep your online presence safe. This book will show you how.

This book begins by discussing major and costly security breaches at corporations and governments to show why cyber security is so important. It then discusses the different types of hackers — helping you get inside a hacker's head — so that you know what you are up against. From there, it details multiple cyber security softwares — including what they are, what they protect you against, and how — that you can invest in to protect yourself online. It moves on to discuss best practices that you can engage in to ensure that you remain safe online. If you follow the guidance presented in these pages, you will both decrease the possibility that hackers will target you and, in the unlikely event that they do, you will be equipped to minimize the damage caused.

Best of luck to you as you take your online safety into your own hands and significantly decrease the chance that you are hit by hackers.

Chapter 1: What is Cyber Security and Why is it Important?

In December 2006, TJX company — the mother company behind stores like TJ Maxx and Marshall's — was hacked so that 94 million of its customers' credit card numbers and identifying information was stolen. For months TJX refused to reveal the size of the breach; it finally disclosed that 45 million credit card numbers were stolen, making it the largest security breach until that time.

At the beginning of 2009, Visa and MasterCard noticed suspicious activity through a myriad of transactions taking place through Heartland Payment Systems. An investigation uncovered that over 130 million credit card numbers had been compromised in a security breach. Heartland Payment Systems was deemed out of compliance by Visa and MasterCard and was not allowed to authorize payments using those cards for several months. The company also had to pay $145 million in compensation for the fraudulent payment activity.

In 2012, hackers reportedly from China broke into the United States Office of Personnel Management system, which contains highly sensitive information on every single individual who is employed by the US government. As the hack was not discovered, the hackers were able to stay inside the system until 2014. During this time, they had access to security clearances, fingerprints, and other critically sensitive information of US government employees. The official report on the security breach claimed that the security of these employees was compromised for a full generation.

In October 2013, the online company Adobe was found to have been hacked. The company originally reported that the hacker stole the encrypted usernames, passwords, and credit card information of three million customers. That number was later reported to be nearly forty million. However, investigators discovered that the hack actually led to 150 million users having their personal and financial information compromised. Adobe had to pay a million dollars.

Around Thanksgiving of 2013, Target's computer system was hacked, and the credit card and contact information — including the full names, email addresses, telephone numbers, and dates of birth —

of over 100 million people was compromised. The hack was not discovered for several weeks, leaving those compromised credit card numbers and identities vulnerable all through the holiday shopping season. The total cost of the hack was estimated at $162 million; as a result, the CEO of Target resigned.

In May 2014, hackers broke into the eBay corporate account using the username and password of three employees. The security breach was not discovered until 229 days later, during which time they had access to the usernames, passwords, dates of birth, and addresses of 145 million users. Fortunately, credit card information was not compromised.

In July 2014, JP Morgan Chase, the largest bank in the United States, fell victim to a hack that affected nearly half of all American households as well as seven small businesses. Although the bank claimed that no money or social security numbers were stolen, the usernames and passwords of many accounts were stolen.

In September 2014, Home Depot announced that it was hacked, probably during the spring of that year; this hack led to the theft of the credit card information of 56 million customers. The hack began when malware masquerading as antivirus software infected the POS systems of the company's stores. The company had to pay nearly twenty million dollars in damages and identity theft protection services to those whose information had been compromised.

In February 2015, the largest security breach in healthcare history occurred when a group of cyber criminals, allegedly sponsored by a foreign government, hacked into the Anthem Health Insurance website. The attack led to millions of names, addresses, dates of birth, and the personal health information of individuals insured by Anthem to become compromised. The breach began when an Anthem employee opened up a phishing email; that one email led to well over one hundred million dollars in damages.

In the fall of 2016, while Yahoo was in negotiations to sell itself to the company Verizon, it disclosed that back in 2014, it had been hacked. 500 million email addresses, real names, dates of birth, and other sensitive information that can lead to identify theft had all been hacked. In the early winter of 2016, it disclosed that it had also been similarly hacked back in 2013. This security breach led to compromising the information of one billion users. Yahoo lost

$350 million in its sell price to Verizon, as well as its good name.

The above information isn't intended to scare you. It's intended to sober you into understanding the importance of cyber security and protecting yourself online. You may be thinking that these are major companies, so of course they will be targeted by hackers. But consider this: companies like Yahoo and Target spend millions and millions of dollars every year in cyber security, yet were still susceptible to security breaches by hackers. Chase Bank spends $250 million on security every year. How much money do you spend every year ensuring that your cyber security is up to date? Probably not nearly as much as these major companies. You are probably way, way more susceptible to a devastating security breach than they ever were.

What is Cyber Security?

Simply put, cyber security is the process whereby you protect yourself online, as well as your entire online presence. It consists of programs that you install on your computer, such as antivirus software or a virtual protected network (VPN), and practices that you may employ on a day-to-day basis, such as guarding your usernames and passwords or keeping a cover on your webcam. Cyber security is intended to protect individuals, companies, computers, networks, programs, and data from unauthorized access of their sensitive information or corrupting files such as viruses, worms, or Trojan horses.

Cyber security does not take a one-size-fits all approach. What works for one computer system may not necessarily provide full protection to another. You can't say that because you installed certain antivirus software, that you are now safe online. Technologies are constantly evolving and growing, at a rate that is so rapid that one can have a difficult time keeping up. Antivirus software that may have protected an older computer that you had five years ago may not protect you adequately on the computer that you have now. An encryption program or VPN that promises to keep you safe online may leave you exposed to undetected threats, possibly those originating in other countries.

Hackers in particular are at the forefront of rapidly evolving technology. They are brilliant computer geeks who may spend hours, days, or even weeks at a time gaining access into other computer systems. Furthermore, they also have an entire underground economy of exploitation codes, botnet services, and other tools of the trade. In this black market, they can buy, sell, and trade with each other to make their hacking exploits even more damaging.

Different Types of Hackers

If you want to really understand cyber security, getting into the mind of a hacker will be beneficial. There is no single one stereotype of a hacker, but they all have two things in common: they are brilliant in regard to technology and have no qualms about breaking into other people's computers. There are several "subtypes" of hackers, so let's break them down.

The Hactivist. A hactivist is a politically motivated hacker who sees his or her hacking activities as promoting justice against oppression. Hactivists tend to work in groups; this method helps them stay anonymous and difficult to trace, as well as enables them to coordinate a large online attack that will be publicly noticed. Possibly the most well-known hactivist group is Anonymous. Anonymous is a group of loosely affiliated individuals who follow ideas and directives to promote their brand of social justice. For example, following the 2014 police shooting of the black man Michael Brown, Anonymous staged what it called "Operation

Ferguson," named after the city where Brown was shot that became home to a series of riots and clashes between civilians and the police. They attacked the Internet and email systems of the City of Ferguson; the Internet went down at City Hall and the phone lines died. Anonymous has engaged in numerous other hacking activities, especially at times of civil unrest. They targeted Israeli computer systems during its assault on Gaza in 2014, as well as terrorist groups such as ISIS and the KKK. The public recognizes them largely by the Guy Fawkes masks, similar to the mask worn by the "terrorist" V in the movie *V for Vendetta*, which they use to symbolize their anonymity and group power. Hactivists can cause significant problems, especially for governments and unjust corporations, by attacking their technological nodes and rallying common people to their causes. Unless you are engaged in political injustice, you probably don't need to worry too much about hactivists.

Cyber criminals. Cyber criminals are probably the hackers that you are most concerned about, and your concerns are well-founded. These are the guys who attack computer systems and networks in order to quickly make a lot of money. Cyber criminals may be exceptionally brilliant high school dropouts, middle-aged men who live in their mothers' basements, or rings of cyber criminals who work together to extort as much money as they can.

There is a full underground economy that cyber criminals use to exchange their tools of the trade. They can buy and sell attack toolkits, exploit codes, and botnet services. They also exploit the personal information of individuals, sometimes selling it for a profit. They may attack individuals or try to bring down entire companies or even governments, all for the sake of earning what they see as easy money. The examples cited at the beginning of the chapter, such as the TJX breach, were hacks committed by cyber criminals.

State-sponsored hackers. Of the three types of hackers, this newly emerging type is probably the most concerning. Governments around the world have found that they can inflict large amounts of damage by paying brilliant hackers buckets of money in order to do their dirty work. They intentionally seek out the best and the brightest, almost like a job search; one might think that state-sponsored hackers are actually government employees.

Because state-sponsored hackers are so well-paid, they have access to an entirely other class of hacking arsenal. Their attacks are undetectable for long periods of time and can sometimes even be unalterable.

Governments may utilize hackers for several different reasons, such as cyber espionage or intellectual theft. In *Operation Aurora,* US officials that Chinese state-sponsored hackers broke into Google, amongst other large, US-based companies, and gained sensitive information on US surveillance as well as intellectual property. In *Operation Stuxnet*, a government, believed to be the US, used state-sponsored hackers to hide viruses on traditional computers, where they hid for years. The believed intention was to target Iran's nuclear program.

In order to stay ahead of hackers, you need a combination of different programs, as well as different well-intentioned efforts to protect your online presence. This book will help you make the best choices you can to protect your own cyber security and, by extension, protect your financial information, identity, and many other critically important things.

Chapter 2: Cyber Security Software

One of your front-line weapons in your battle to protect your own cyber security is the software that you use to keep your computer safe. This chapter will explore different types of software that you can use, as well as how you can choose the best of each kind.

Access Control

Access control is a method by which only a selected number of individuals or users are authorized to access a certain resource. One of the most common forms of access control in cyber security is the use of login credentials. Login credentials means that a user presents his or her credentials in order to gain access to the system. This may be in the form of a username and password, or it could be a more high-tech system, such as requiring that a user swipe a key card, scan a fob, or present a fingerprint or retina scan. If the individual's credentials check out, then he or she is granted access into the system.

The easiest form of access control that you can implement on your own computer is requiring that a password be entered before a user can log on. This will protect your computer, as well as the sensitive information stored on it, from prying eyes. On your desktop itself, you should also consider requiring a password to open files that contain sensitive information, such as the file that contains your usernames and passwords.

However, simply requiring a password will not be enough should your computer fall into the hands of hackers. Keep reading to see how else you can protect yourself.

Anti Key-loggers

Anti key-logging software is designed to prevent or disable the use of key-logging software. Key-logging software is software that records the pattern in which keys on a keyboard are struck. Usually key-logging software is covert, so the individual being recorded is unaware. Key-logging software may be included in a malware package that is downloaded onto a computer without the owner of the computer's knowledge; hackers can use it to easily gain access to a computer or a system used by the computer's user by recording information typed in such as usernames, passwords, and credit card numbers.

Anti key-logging software detects key-logging software and either deletes it or immobilizes it so that it cannot be used on the computer. There are two basic types of anti key-logging software: signature-based and heuristic-based. Signature-based anti key-logging software has a long, developed list of key-logging software, as well as ways to easily identify if such software is being used. It then disables the software so that it is not able to record the keystrokes on a computer. Heuristic-based anti key-logging software doesn't have a list of key-logging software but rather maintains an analysis regarding the different features that key-logging software is known to have. Both types of software have benefits and drawbacks.

Companies such as financial institutions invest heavily in anti key-logging software, especially to protect the entering of information such as PINs. You can expect to pay $30 to $50 a year if you want to download anti key-logging software onto your own personal computer. Some top-of-the-line anti-virus software will also include anti key-logging software.

Anti-Malware

Malware is a rather ubiquitous term, and while most people understand that it is generally bad, they aren't entirely sure of what it means. "Malware" is short for "malicious software," and it is used to refer to any type of intrusive program that can damage or permanently disable your computer. This includes viruses, Trojan horses, worms, ransomware, and adware.

Anti-malware software is commonly referred to as anti-virus. It is designed to prevent, detect, and remove any form of malware before it gains access to your computer. Anti-malware was originally created to remove viruses, but now that there has been a proliferation of other forms of malware, it can protect users against things such as key-logging software, ransomware, Trojan horses, and any other types of malware. Some anti-malware also protects users from malicious URLs and spam emails that can contain malware. Sometimes the user is notified that the information he or she is about to access may be malicious and given the option of accessing it anyways; sometimes, the user is completely prevented from being able to access any malicious information.

Some anti-malware software is free, so a lot of individuals are tempted to skimp out on protection.

However, free anti-malware is not the best quality. In fact, some free anti-malware kits actually turn into viruses after they expire! You need to plan to make a small financial investment every year in high-quality anti-malware. If you have a PC, there are many options from which to choose, based on your budget and what your own security needs are. If you have a Mac, your computer is already equipped with built-in anti-malware. However, you will want to also download additional protection, such as MacKeeper, to keep your system running optimally.

You will want to run a system scan with your anti-malware at least once every month. If you are a gamer, download a lot, or access movie websites, you will want to scan it significantly more often.

Anti-Spyware

Spyware is software that hackers use to gain information from computer users without their knowledge. In other words, they spy on them. They can use spyware to try to access sensitive information such as credit card numbers, social security numbers, and other personal identifying information that can compromise a person's identity. This information can then either be used directly by the hacker or be sent to a third-party for a profit. The thought that your computer could be infected with this particularly malicious form of malware should send shivers up your spine!

Anti-spyware software is designed to either remove or block spyware, or to prevent it from being able to enter into a computer system in the first place. Many anti-malware packages include anti-spyware; for this reason, you should invest in a high quality, top-of-the-line anti-malware. If your anti-malware does not include anti-spyware, you need to invest in anti-spyware today.

Anti-spyware works in two ways. The first way is by scanning all of the network data that comes into a system to see if it contains any known form of spyware and any other related threats. The second way is by removing or blocking any spyware that may already be present. If your anti-spyware works in the second way, then you absolutely must scan your computer on a regular schedule to ensure that the spyware is dealt with before it causes catastrophic damage.

Some spyware cannot be removed with regular anti-spyware, especially if multiple large pieces of software have gained access to a Windows-based computer. If this happens, you will need to take your computer to a trained and certified specialist to have all of the data backed up and the operating system completely re-installed. This process may be quite costly, which is why you should invest money in anti-spyware sooner to keep from having to pay more later.

Anti-Subversion Software

Subversion software is a software that subverts the normal code on which a program is intended to run. It can do this for the purpose of corrupting the data stored in a system (possibly to protect an individual that the data may incriminate, or for any other nefarious reason), theft, and allowing unauthorized access into a system. Subversion software is a favorite tool used by hackers to corrupt programs.

Anti-subversion software stops subversion software and attempts to reverse it. It accomplishes this job through two primary ways. The first is called static anti-subversion. Static anti-subversion is created while the code itself is being created to ensure that the code cannot be corrupted. Dynamic anti-subversion, the second way, is carried out while the code is being executed and continually checks for unintended results of the code being carried out.

Anti-subversion software is a must if you are writing any kind of computer code, be it for yourself, for a company, or for an app that you want to develop because you think that it will benefit people. Software codes can be subverted at any point throughout their lifecycle, not just while they are being created, so protecting them is of the utmost importance. Protecting the codes that you create is tantamount to protecting your own good name.

Anti-Tamper Software

Anti-tamper software essentially applies tamper resistance to any kind of software; therefore, attackers have a much more difficult time attempting to modify it. Tampering is a malicious activity associated with hacking and is usually done with the assistance of rootkits and backdoors. Rootkits are computer software that allow users to gain access to areas that would not otherwise be accessible, possibly because they do not have the right credentials (hence the need for high-quality access credentials). Backdoors are secret methods of avoiding authentication to gain access to a system and are used by hackers to remotely hack into a computer.

Tampering can take the form of installing rootkits or backdoors, installing malware, or disabling security monitoring, amongst other things. It causes the software that it gains access to become corrupted.

Anti-tampering software prevents hackers from being able to tamper with the software on your computer system. The two types of anti-tampering software are external anti-tampering and internal anti-tampering. External anti-tampering monitors software to detect whether or not tampering has occurred and usually comes in the form of anti-malware software; it is the kind that is most easily and readily accessible to general users. Internal anti-tampering causes the software in question to become its own security system, usually through a code. This form of anti-tampering software is used more often by coders and large organizations. Some anti-tamper technology utilizes encryption or other cryptographic software to prevent hackers from being able to view the codes used in software.

Many large companies, especially financial institutions, protect themselves by using anti-tampering software. Look and see if your anti-malware has anti-tampering software as one of its benefits. If not, you may want to invest in some.

Cryptographic Software

Cryptographic or encryption software utilizes encryption to prevent unauthorized access to a digital system. Encryption is the practice of hiding or disguising information that is intended to be sent electronically. The practice is as old as long-distance communications; back in ancient times, couriers would commonly carry messages that were encrypted so that, if they were apprehended on the route, no one would be able to decipher the message. As soon as electronic messages were able to be sent through long distances, encryption was employed. During World War I and World War II, hundreds, if not thousands, of cryptographers were hired to decipher messages that were intercepted from enemy communications.

Nowadays, encryption is much more advanced and sophisticated so as to keep pace with rapidly evolving technology. It usually uses complex algorithms to keep from being detected and deciphered by unwanted third parties. People and companies use encryption to make sure that the information that they send electronically is not intercepted or, if it is, that it is not readable. Hackers are constantly trying to access information that is sent electronically, so using encryption software is a good way to protect yourself.

Encryption software uses something called a cipher to transform the meaningful message that was originally sent into something called ciphertext, which resembles gobbledygook. The intended recipient of the message is able to read the original, meaningful message as it was originally sent. However, if anyone else tries to access it, it will not make any sense.

There are many software products that enable encryption. One of the easiest methods of utilizing encryption software is to go to your email account settings and set them to encrypt your emails. This simple measure will help prevent them from being intercepted by unwanted third parties. Below are some other types of encryption software.

Virtual Protected Network (VPN). A VPN is a type of encryption software that changes the location of your computer's ISP address. This is a particularly handy tool to use when traveling, as it prevents the governments and any ne'er-do-wells of other countries from being able to access your information. For example, if you are traveling in Brazil, you can set your VPN to say that you are in

California. All of your Internet traffic will appear to originate in California, making it impossible to track.

Some VPNs are completely free. Others may cost around $50 a year. Look for one that best meets your needs.

VPNs are a great way to protect yourself, but they can only do so much. They can't protect the local files on your computer, and unless you are using secure HTTPS sites, the traffic between the VPN server and your computer is not secure. For these reasons, you need to use more than a VPN.

Built-in Encryption Software. In 2015 when two shooters rampaged a health center in San Bernardino, California, the FBI asked Apple to provide a back door to enable them to get into the attackers' iPhones. Apple completely refused and would not back down. One reason why is because creating a backdoor would compromise the cryptographic software that was already present in all of their products. The cryptographic software was so strong that the FBI took over three months attempting to unlock the phone.

Look into what built-in encryption software your computer, tablet, or phone came with. If you need to supplement it with any additional encryption software (other than a VPN, which is a must!), make sure that you are doing so in such a way that will enhance the security features already present.

Blockchain. Blockchain is a type of software that was originally designed to host the virtual currency known as Bitcoin. Since its inception in 2008, its potential has been exploited to create a host of software products that provide a high level of encryption. Blockchain uses public-key encryption and a high-accountability system of node computers to provide some of the best security features in the world of cyber security. Many are now saying that blockchain is the future of encryption software.

Many companies, especially financial institutions, are experimenting with blockchain to see how its security features can protect them and their customers. While developing your own blockchain is an inaccessible method of upping your own cyber security, one thing that you can do to take advantage of blockchain is try to only use the websites of companies that use blockchain. See if your bank's website uses blockchain; if it does, your financial information will likely never be compromised.

Blocknet is essentially an entirely new Internet whose applications run entirely on blockchain technology. You can look into how you can use blocknet to help ensure that the information that you send digitally is always encrypted.

The above are just a few of the different types of encryption software that you can look into. Windows, Linux, and other operating systems have other encryption software that are available directly from the operating system company and are designed to protect both your local information as well as information that you send digitally.

Firewall

A firewall is a cyber security system which carefully controls and monitors all incoming and outgoing traffic. It does so by creating a barrier between a secure system and a system that is understood to generally be insecure, such as the Internet.

There are two types of firewalls: host-based firewalls and network firewalls. A host-based firewall is a layer of software on the host computer that controls all of the traffic that goes to and from the host. A network firewall is software that runs on general-purpose hardware and filters all traffic between two different networks. A firewall can also create a VPN for the computer on which it operates.

Intrusion Detection System (IDS)

Intrusion detection system (IDS) is a blanket term for computer software that monitors a system for any kind of suspicious activity. The information about the suspicious activity is then sent to the computer's administrator or to a security information and event management (SIEM) database for inspection.

One form of it is probably very familiar to you already: antivirus protection. There are two basic types of IDS: network intrusion detection system (NIDS) and host-based intrusion detection system (HIDS). An NIDS system monitors incoming traffic to make sure that it is free from threats. An HIDS system monitors all of the files within an operating system.

Intrusion Prevention System (IPS)

An intrusion prevention system, or IPS, is a type of IDS that has the capability of responding to any threats or malicious activity that is detected. When any suspicious activity is detected, it immediately blocks it. Not only does it monitor and log any threats, but it also can analyze problems associated with a company's security policies and discourage individuals from violating those policies.

An IPS might use one or more of different detection and response methods. One is called stateful protocol analysis detection, and it uses observed and recorded activity, which is considered to be benign, in order to determine activity that is out of the ordinary and therefore suspicious. Another is called signature-based detection, and it looks for the signatures of software that are known to be malicious. A potential drawback of signature-based detection is that it may not be as effective against new threats that are not already established with signatures. Statistical anomaly-based detection is the third kind. Statistical anomaly-based detection is a method by which the system searches for anomalies or aberrations based on known patterns of benign use.

Sandbox

A sandbox is a useful way to test out a program that is potentially dangerous without running the risk of harming the entire computer. It allows a program to be carried out using a controlled amount of the computer's resources, so if the program has, say, a defective code or has a virus embedded in it, the damage will be limited to the computer's resources that were used to run it. Therefore, all of the sensitive information stored on the computer will remain safe, even if the file proves to be malicious.

Sandboxes can be extremely useful for large corporations or for individuals who download a lot of information from the Internet. Using them can prevent catastrophic damage to the entire computer system.

Security Information Management

Security information management refers to the composite collection of data so that it can be analyzed. An example would be a log of times that an account was accessed and the places from which such access occurred. The information is then sent to a centralized computer server, from which it can be accessed by people who have the proper credentials. This type of information can be extremely useful in an investigation, should a hack occur. It can help immediately detect suspicious activity, thereby possibly preventing a hack before it even begins.

Companies that are serious about cyber security need to invest in some form of security information management. This will ensure that should a breach ever happen, they will have a better chance of being able to track down the source of the hack (the cyber-criminal or hacker behind it) and prosecute to the fullest extent of the law.

SIEM

SIEM stands for security information and event management. It refers to software or an outside, managed service that logs security data, provides analysis of security threats in real time, and generates compliance reports. SIEM is commonly used by companies that deal with large amounts of data, which needs to be constantly monitored and protected in real time.

Some companies choose to use software to meet their SIEM needs, while others choose to use an outside company. The outside company will have access to your computer's information so that it can monitor and analyze the computer's use and any security threats. Using an outside company may be more expensive than software. However, the company will probably provide some kind of insurance should a security breach occur in which it covers the damage caused by the breach.

Protecting your company's data and the personal information of your company's customers and clients is supremely important to both your bottom line and reputation, so a good SIEM system or company is definitely worth the investment.

Chapter 3: Cyber Security Best Practices

In addition to ensuring that you are properly protected with the necessary software, there are other best practices that you can engage in to best keep you safe online and protect you from hackers. While there is never a 100% guarantee that you absolutely will not be targeted by hackers, following these best practices will help increase the difficulty of hacking into your computer. Hopefully, any hacker who may target you will see that you have layers of protection and will decide to move on to someone who is not as protected as you are.

Use Difficult Passwords

Many times, hackers target online accounts that are password protected. One of the easiest ways for them to gain access is for you to have easy passwords. In addition, unscrupulous family, friends, or co-workers may try to break into your accounts by trying to guess what your passwords are.

Many people use common things for their passwords, such as their favorite foods, the name of one of their children, the name of their significant other, favorite plants or animals, a nickname, or the name of a pet. Other common passwords include a series of numbers such as 123456789 or variations of "password." These passwords are way too obvious! If you have a password such as one of the above, anyone who knows you well will be able to easily figure it out, especially if you have a password hint. Then, your password is a dead giveaway.

Use a difficult combination of numbers, letters, and symbols to create difficult passwords that people will not be able to crack. A password such as "fvx06997!?" will be much, much more difficult to figure out than "justinsgirl."

Don't Reuse Passwords

Many people don't even think about using different passwords for different accounts. After all, having multiple passwords makes keeping track of them difficult. Having just one password means that you can log into all of your accounts with ease, without even having to think about what the password is. However, this could potentially open you up to hackers compromising your accounts.

Having multiple passwords is understandably challenging. You may insist that your password for your email account is asdf1234kjb, but that is actually the password for your Facebook account. The frustration and anxiety created by not being able to keep up with multiple passwords can either make you give up or drive you to the brink of your sanity. However, reusing passwords for multiple accounts makes hacking into your accounts easier. If someone figures out the password into just one of those accounts, that person may have access to your email, Facebook, bank account, Amazon account, the list goes on. By the time the damage is discovered, you could be out hundreds or even thousands of dollars, as well as have embarrassing pictures posted on your social media.

One way to make the challenge of having multiple passwords easier is to keep a document of passwords on your desktop or phone. Beware, though. Make sure that this document is encrypted and password-protected. If anybody was to gain access to it, all of your accounts could be compromised.

Frequently Change Passwords

Some people never change their passwords. Ever. Even if they get locked out of an account and are requested to change their passwords to protect their security, they either refuse to do so or, after changing it, immediately change it back to what it was. This action is understandable. After all, you may have your email login information saved onto your own devices, and then when you need to access your email from another computer, you may not have any idea what you changed your password to. You may either have to change your password altogether or just give up on trying to log in from a different computer. The process is enough to frustrate anyone.

However, not changing your passwords can be just as damaging as using the same password for multiple accounts. At any given time, somebody may be on the brink of deciphering one of your passwords. Imagine that someone was able to figure out the password to your online bank account and was able to access it!

As a rule of thumb, you need to change your passwords at least every six months. Anytime you get an email suggesting that unauthorized activity may have been carried out on an account, you need to change that account's password right away. If you must use password recovery to get into an account that you are locked out of, do not change your password into an old, previously used password.

Don't Share Passwords

Never, ever, ever let anyone — save for possibly your significant other, and even then, many people don't share their passwords — know what your passwords are. The temptation to access your online accounts and use them for personal gain and benefit may prove to be too much for even the most scrupulous friends.

The fact is that you are responsible for any activity under your accounts. If fraudulent activity occurs, you may be responsible for it until you can prove that someone else accessed your account without your permission.

Sometimes, you may need to give a trusted friend a password so that he or she can access information for you while you are not able. In that event, you need to change your password as soon as that friend no longer needs to access your information. You also need to closely monitor all activity into and out of that account. Politely thank your friend for his or her assistance and then let him or her know that you will be changing the password.

Use a VPN

A VPN is a virtual protected network, and using one anytime you are browsing online has multiple benefits in regard to your online security. If you are on a public Internet server, such as one at Starbucks, a hotel, or any other public place, there is likely no encryption provided, making any information that you send available to a hacker that would take the time to try to access it. And many, many hackers will take the time to try to access it! A VPN can prevent this scenario because it reroutes all of your Internet browsing through a private server, making it inaccessible to private eyes.

Another benefit of a VPN is that you can access websites without being watched by a third party, such as a government entity. This is possible because you can set your VPN to route all of your Internet browsing through a server in a foreign country. If you are traveling, some countries censor certain websites, especially those that involve any kind of governmental dissent. Using a VPN will allow you to gain full access to all of those websites.

Yet another benefit of using a VPN is that you can protect your VOIP calls, such as those made over Skype or FaceTime. VOIP calls are so easy to access that even a novice hacker can break into them. The thought that someone else is listening in on your private phone calls can be unnerving at best and dangerous at worst, especially if you are sharing any kind of confidential information that you don't want other people to be privy to.

Another benefit of using a VPN is that when you use a search engine, such as Google or Yahoo!, your searches won't be recorded. Any time you run a search through a search engine, that search gets saved under your name. For example, if you use Google to perform a search on a device that is authorized to access your Gmail account, anytime you access your Gmail account on a different device, the results of that search will follow you. This is so that you don't have to re-enter previous searches (it's meant to be a convenient for you) and so that ads can better target potential customers. However, some of your searches may be a little bit embarrassing. If you search for dating advice and then that search re-appears on your date's laptop when you use it to access your email, you may be a bit embarrassed! Some scenarios are not embarrassing but actually dangerous, especially if you are in a line of work that requires you to research difficult topics such as war crimes or brothels. Using a VPN will prevent your searches from being recorded.

Perhaps the most important reason to always use a VPN is because privacy is a right that has lately turned into a commodity. Very few people actually experience online privacy because their every move online can be tracked, either by hackers or the government. If you believe that privacy is a right that is worth protecting, then you need to make sure that you are always, ALWAYS using a VPN.

Use a Credit Protection Service, Such as LifeLock

Most financial transactions that occur nowadays are digital. Whereas twenty years ago you may have had to write a check and wait for a couple of days for it to clear the bank, nowadays, you just swipe a debit or credit card and the transaction appears immediately. Whereas twenty years ago applying for a credit card may have taken weeks, considering that processing the application may have involved going through mountains of paperwork, nowadays, you can be approved in 60 seconds. Hackers are finding more and more clever ways to access your financial information so that they can make an easy, untraceable buck. Protecting your financial information online is of the utmost importance.

While these high-speed digital transactions are certainly convenient, they can leave you extremely vulnerable to identity theft and credit card fraud. If someone gains access to your personal information, as happened during many of the security breaches mentioned at the beginning of this book, that person can easily apply for a credit card in your name. You may have no idea that your identity was stolen and someone else is making purchases that you are financially responsible for until months or even years later. During that time, the damage can add up to hundreds of thousands of dollars.

One way to protect yourself is to use a credit protection service. Services such as LifeLock will notify you any time an application for any financial account, such as a new bank account or credit card, is made. The application will not be approved unless you give your consent, verifying that you, the owner of the personal information used, authorized the application. This can be a valuable way of protecting you from identity theft and protecting your financial information in the digital age.

Credit protection services are not free, and there are other methods of protecting your good name online without paying for one. One method is to place a security freeze on your credit report. Depending on the laws for security freezes in your state, no credit application will be approved as long as you have a security freeze in place. There is a small fee associated with a security freeze — typically around $10 — but if you are the victim of identity theft, you may be able to get it for free.

Another method is to place a fraud alert on your credit report. A fraud alert will notify you anytime your credit score is accessed. You can then determine whether you were the one to access your credit score and know immediately if someone is trying to steal your identity. Fraud alerts typically last for 90 days, so they need to be frequently renewed. However, if you have been the victim of identity theft, you can apply for a long-term fraud alert that will last for seven years.

You are entitled to receive a free copy of your credit report every year from each of the three credit reporting agencies. Make sure that you take advantage of this service by requesting a free copy of your credit report every four months from a different agency. Carefully review the information to make sure that no fraudulent activity has occurred. If there is anything suspicious on your credit report, immediately notify the credit bureau before further damage is done.

If you are truly passionate about cyber security, you may want to invest in multiple forms of credit protection, such as enlisting the assistance of a credit protection service as well as using other methods such as a security freeze.

Cover Your Webcam

In 2016, James Comey, then-director of the FBI, recommended that all private citizens cover their webcams on their phones, computers, and tablets. Hackers, government agencies, and other entities have developed ways to use webcams to spy on people using their devices. In 2010, Harriton High School in Pennsylvania used webcams on school-issued laptops to take pictures of the people who were using them. They were programmed to take a picture every 15 minutes as a way of verifying the identity of the user. One student found that the laptop he was using had taken 400 pictures of him, including some when he was either asleep or partially dressed. The school only narrowly escaped having to face criminal charges for its actions. What is scary is that it was able to use the webcams for this purpose.

Nefarious individuals have been found to use webcams to spy on unsuspecting women in order to take pictures of them in the nude. Some have even sold webcams that are programmed to do this. What is particularly distressing is that hackers that use these specially programmed webcams can disable the light that tells the computer's user that the webcam is on. Therefore, that person has no idea that he or she is being spied on. Some particularly unscrupulous individuals will then use the videos to blackmail or extort the victims.

The easiest way to cover your webcam is to do what Facebook CEO Mark Zuckerberg does: cover it with a piece of dark tape. Whenever you want to use your webcam to make a video call, remove the tape. After the call is over, apply another piece of tape. Imagine that something so simple as a small piece of tape could protect your online privacy and even prevent you from being blackmailed or extorted! But a hacker will not be able to override this physical obstruction.

Log Out of Your Desktop

This best practice should be a no-brainer if you are using a public computer, such as one at school or work. However, you should always log out of your desktop, even on your own personal computer. It is not unheard of for hackers to be able to gain access to your desktop, even if you are not currently using it and/or it is asleep.

Getting into somebody else's desktop is like hacking 101. If you are online, then a novice hacker doesn't even need black-market software to be able to gain entry to your desktop while you are online. Once you are no longer on your computer, if your desktop is still logged in, then the hacker has free reign of your computer. You may come back and find that you have been hit with viruses, that all of your passwords have been compromised, and/or that all of your important files have been deleted.

Be Wary of Unknown Emails and External Downloads

Phishing, which is the practice of sending fraudulent emails in order to extract personal and/or sensitive information, is an increasingly common practice in today's digital world. Hackers and online thieves are always looking for ways to get your information, and one way that they try is to send legitimate-looking emails.

A common email scam is for someone, sometimes a deposed royal, to contact you asking for financial help. If you allow your sympathetic response to be activated by this plea, you will run yourself into a heap of trouble. People and organizations that you don't know and/or are not affiliated with that send emails asking for financial help often have a way of being able to track the bank account information for any incoming transaction. What this means is that if you even send one dollar in response to an email asking for help, the person or entity that sent that email may be able to reverse engineer the information to the bank account from which that money was sent. You could be out your entire bank account before you even know what happened! As a general rule of thumb, do not EVER send money to someone that you do not know, especially not over the Internet. If you absolutely cannot resist, use a third-party payment system such as PayPal. That way, the money that you send will not directly lead to your bank account.

A variation of this scam is that someone may ask you if you can cash a check for him or her in return for an inordinately large amount of money. In return, you are requested to either provide a small service or give him or her a small portion of the money sent. Do not ever accept money for something that you have not done! The criminal could use this scheme to gain access to your bank account.

On that note, an ad claiming that you are a winner is not ever legitimate. Don't ever click on it! You are not going to get a free prize, unless you consider some form of malware getting downloaded onto your computer to be a prize.

Another method of phishing that online criminals like to use is to get you to download a file that looks legitimate. They may do so by posing as a friend or a legitimate organization, even the company that you work for! Without even questioning who the sender is, you will open the email that they sent. Attached may be a file that looks completely legitimate but is actually a spyware program. Before you know it, your computer is infected with spyware! One of the scariest things about spyware is you may *never* know that your computer has been infected. It will continue to operate normally, because there is no presence of a virus or other bug to cause problems. However, someone is now spying on everything that you do over the computer. Many companies have policies that state that employees may not open email attachments, even from trusted senders, to prevent this scenario. You may want to consider adopting this policy. There are usually alternatives to sending attachments, such as sending links to webpages or sending something via a cloud service such as Google Docs. To further protect yourself, make absolutely certain that your computer is equipped with spyware protection. Only a high-quality spyware protection program will be able to detect and eliminate spyware that may have infected your computer.

Another phishing scam is that a bogus cyber security expert may claim that your computer is infected and that he or she needs to gain remote access in order to fix the problem. If your computer is truly infected, so badly that your antivirus and other security software is unable to fix the problem, you need to take your computer to a trusted computer repair service. Do not ever let a third party gain remote access to your computer unless you initiated the conversation. For example, if you have contacted tech support for a computer application, such as Skype, the tech may need to gain remote access. In that situation, granting such access is okay because you initiated the conversation. However, if someone claiming to be from Skype contacts you to let you know that your computer may be infected, absolutely do not respond to the email and do NOT let this person gain access to your computer! Instead, immediately contact Skype to let its staff know that someone is phishing by claiming to be from Skype.

Always Be on The Lookout for Security Breaches

This best practice has two aspects, private and corporate. Always stay up-to-date on the transactions that are occurring with your bank account and credit card. If you notice anything suspicious, take action right away. If you do not regularly monitor your financial information, you may not catch fraudulent activity for weeks, months, or even years after a hacker first got into your accounts. By that time, the damage could be so extensive that you may never recover.

You also need to constantly be on the lookout for corporate security breaches. For example, if you have a credit card with a major retailer and find that that retailer suffered a security breach, such as one of those mentioned at the beginning of this book, you need to take immediate action to minimize or even reverse the damage that you may potentially sustain. Immediately request a new credit card with new numbers. Be prepared for the fact that your social security number, date of birth, real name, address, and phone number may have already been compromised. If you are unaware that your bank was hacked, or a company with which you hold a credit card, you could be ignorant of the fact that you are losing hundreds or even thousands of dollars to a hacker.

Back Up Your Data

Sometimes, hackers come in and wipe all of the information from your computer system. If this happens, you don't want this to be a total loss or catastrophe. Whether you are an individual, a small business owner, or in charge of your department at a large corporation, having all of your data wiped from your computer system can cause an inordinate amount of loss. You can spend a lot of time and money trying to regain only a fraction of what you originally had.

One method of ensuring that the damage done in case your computer gets wiped clean is minimized is to back up your data on a regular basis. You can do this with an external hard drive or through a cloud-based service. If you choose to use a cloud-based service, make sure that it is heavily encrypted and has a high reputation for being secure. Choose a unique username and password that cannot be easily traced to you. If you use a hard drive to back up your data, make sure that you keep it under lock and key. The last thing that you want is to go through the effort of protecting your data by backing it up, only to find that a hacker is able to access it through the back door.

Make Sure Your Programs Are Up to Date

Very few people feel a rush of adrenaline when they see a notification on their computers saying that updates need to be installed. Going through the process of restarting your computer so that the updates can be installed, especially when you have 12 Internet tabs open and are working on a major project, can be disruptive. However, you need to always make sure that your programs are up to date. One reason is that whenever updates are made available, they almost always include new security features that will help protect you and the information that you have stored in those programs.

You especially want to make sure that you keep your security programs, such as antivirus, updated. While most antivirus programs are renewed every year, viruses, spyware, and other forms of malware are not created on a schedule that corresponds with your updates and renewals. Updates may be available that protect you against new threats that could bring down your entire system. If an update is available for your antivirus, make sure that you install it immediately.

Use Pop-Up Blockers

Pop-ups are those pesky little windows that appear at times when you click on links. Sometimes, they appear when you didn't even click on anything! They usually say something to the effect of you winning a large prize in a contest that you know nothing about. Pop-ups are usually nothing but bad news. More than just being annoying, they can quickly infect your computer with all kinds of malware before you even know what happened.

Fortunately, you can easily protect yourself against pernicious pop-ups by disabling them. Your operating system and Internet browser probably have their own unique method of disabling pop-ups. If you use Google Chrome, go to Settings on the Chrome toolbar. Click on Advanced Settings, then Privacy, then Content. Under Pop-ups, make sure that you have selected the option that says, "Do not allow any site to show pop-ups (recommended)."

You can then manage exceptions for times in which you will allow pop-ups.

Keep Your Antivirus On

Do not ever turn your antivirus off! If you are trying to access a website or program that requires you to turn off your antivirus, it is probably asking you to do so because it wants to infect your computer with malware. Always, always, always keep your antivirus and other protective software, such as firewalls, on. Do not ever disable them for any reason.

On that note, make sure that you scan your computer for viruses on a regular schedule, at least one time every month. Depending on the websites that you visit, you may want to do so more often.

Don't Visit Pornography Websites

No type of website is designed to load your computer with more malware than a pornography website. Even if your pop-up blocker is enabled, multiple pop-ups will come up any time that you click your mouse. Each of those pop-ups potentially holds viruses, Trojan horses, worms, spyware, the list goes on. Furthermore, both hackers and the people who are running the website are more prone than owners of other websites to spy on you with your own webcam. Afterwards, your antivirus may blatantly say that because you visited a pornographic website, your computer became infected. Few things will infect your computer faster than a visit to a pornographic website.

If you are using a work computer, visiting a pornography website can easily get you fired. If you are using a personal computer, visiting a pornography website can quickly infect your computer with so much malware that you may have to pay a visit to a technician. This could prove to be both expensive and embarrassing.

Use Secure Wi-Fi

Public Wi-Fi connections are not secure; hackers can easily get into the network to see what traffic is coming in and out of them. A more experienced hacker will be able to use the information he finds to glean important personal information from you, potentially leading to identity theft. Using a secure Wi-Fi connection involves using a VPN and so much more.

Whenever possible, avoid using a public Wi-Fi connection. If you do use public Wi-Fi, make sure it is a connection that requires you to log in with a username and password. This provides a layer of security, which will cause hackers to have a more difficult time to access your Internet traffic. And if you make a hacker's job more difficult, you stand a greater chance that he or she will move on to the next victim.

If you are using a connection that is not your personal home connection, including Internet at work, always use a VPN. This will keep unscrupulous coworkers, some of whom may be hackers themselves, from accessing the information that you send over the Internet. It will also make any Internet traffic difficult to trace back to you.

If you are running a business or are in charge of your department's Internet connection, make sure that the Internet is secure and encrypted. To find out how to do this, call the Internet company. The package may cost a little more every month, but the extra cost will be well worth it. You could very well save yourself time and energy from having to deal with a costly and time-consuming hack.

Wipe Data from Old Devices

Before you take your old smart phone, tablet, or computer to the Geek Squad or other computer center for recycling, you need to first wipe all of the data. The memory stored on your device is easily accessible by virtually anyone who is skilled in computer repair, even the scrupulous Geek Squadders. Who is to say that one of them isn't in a desperate place and needs an easy way to make a few extra dollars? They could easily take the memory from your computer's hard drive, take it home, find the information necessary to steal your identity, and have all of the computer smarts to hide the evidence.

There are tools and methods that you can use to wipe your old devices. You can completely erase all of the data from your device using destruction software, which is what government agencies such as the Department of Defense do. Some destruction software, such as Disk Wipe, is completely free. You could degauss your hard drive. Degaussing is a process whereby you so severely disrupt the magnetic field that the information stored in it becomes so scrambled that it is virtually inaccessible. You could also destroy the hard drive. Whatever method you choose, make sure that when you hand your device over for recycling, you do not leave yourself susceptible to having your personal information compromised.

Scan All Devices

In today's hyperconnected world, many devices can be plugged into your computer. Your smart phone probably can be plugged into your computer to access updates and sync with apps and documents stored on your computer. You may have a tablet that can do the same thing. An e-reader, such as a Kindle, can be plugged into a computer in order to download ebooks that are on your desktop, without an Internet connection. A USB or external hard drive can be plugged into your computer to enable you to view files that may not be saved on your desktop. You can also charge a lot of devices by plugging them into your computer.

In the process of getting the most out of your gadgets by plugging them into your computer, you may actually be infecting your computer with viruses. Any of your auxiliary devices, such as your e-reader or USB drive, could potentially be infected with malware and you not even know it. Make sure that you always scan any device that you plug into your computer. Your antivirus software should have an option to do this; usually, as soon as you plug something in, a dialogue box will pop up asking if you want to scan the external device. Always select yes. Your antivirus could detect and remove any threats, thereby keeping not only your computer clean but also any devices.

On that note, don't let anybody else plug a device into your computer. You have no idea what malicious files may be stored on them, and you don't want those files to gain access to your computer. Especially not when you have worked so hard to protect your own cyber security!

Similarly, you should never plug one of your devices into a public computer. You do not know what that computer may be infected with, and just like a biological infection, any present malware could find its way from that computer to your device and, from there, onto your personal computer. Keep your gadgets to yourself.

Conclusion

In conclusion, cyber security is something that everyone can practice in order to keep themselves safe from hackers. It is important for companies to practice cyber security, in order to protect not only themselves but also the customers that they service. Problems with cyber security can lead to costly and time-consuming breaches that can wreak havoc on a company and sometimes even destroy its reputations. With individuals, important data and personal information can be compromised, leading to identity theft. You cannot take cyber security too seriously; failing to use adequate protection can be catastrophic, causing damage that can take years to repair.

Your cyber security is essentially in your own hands. This news should be welcome, because there is so much that you can do to protect yourself online. You can invest in software that detects and removes malicious threats from your computer, such as spyware, adware, viruses, rootkits, and backdoors. These are common things that hackers use in order to access your computer, so making sure that your computer stays free of them is your first line of defense in keeping yourself online. You can also make sure that you always use a VPN, keep your antivirus activated and updated, keep your webcam covered, and make sure that your Internet connections are secure, just to name a few of the cyber security best practices that you can utilize.

Employing cyber security tactics will not guarantee 100% that you will not be targeted by hackers. After all, hackers have managed to get into accounts run by the United States government. However, you can severely minimize the probability that you will be targeted. By making yourself a more difficult target, you raise the possibility that the cyber-criminal will give up on you and move on to an easier target.